On the Occasion of a Wedding

.

To Kristi and Matthew —

WHO ARE RECEIVING THIS BOOK
AS A WEDDING GIFT INSTEAD OF SOMETHING
MORE PRACTICAL OFF THEIR REGISTRY

its sting
is what makes
it beautiful

AMOR INSANUS

PLUIT ET LUCET

PROEM

Morning awakes in secret
    to kiss the golden marigolds.

The sun is spreading its warmth;
    the air is fragrant,
    the spirit light,
    the heart is overjoyed.

Myself, wholly revealed;
    how lovely His light pours from my body.

—

I write a great book of remembrance,
    recording all things seen, heard, and felt;
    all love is entered in its fullness,
    and nothing is omitted.

—

May I never forsake Him;
    through the whole of my life
    may I honor Him.

Flores Caelesti

heavenly flowers

QUANTA QUALIA

i've spent years contemplating
how to adequately describe
the raw feeling of you

but no combination of
one hundred thousand words
can capture even
the slightest quanta

do we love, or
am I but a blue tangerine?

the answer
the reality
no longer matter

for I was unconscious before you
and now I am divine

BREATH OF TUOLUMNE

I dwell in a meadow where
    the wild tarragon grows, amidst unwanted butterweeds,
    and rocky granite outcrops.

Oak leaves fall like blessings all around me.

I press life between the pages of poems.
    I brew tea inside the murmur of streams.

Oh lonesome wildwood —
    How did love come to master my soul?

Fortitude is the fragrance that drops from the cows,
    and I breathe him in. Always, always him.

Rose Haiku of the Newlyweds

virgin buds fading
under sun's burning passion
ashes of roses

—

my morning's first smile
his soft sigh of love
whispering roses

—

two drunk kakakul birds
passing vitals between beaks
love's liqueur of rose

—

feathering our nest
we choose goose down and petals
no sharp bed of thorns

Hafiz Love Knot

Two souls knit together.
Two lives become but one.

Former wills must sever;
Neither right nor wrong.

Cords of life entangled,
With humbled threads consigned—

How can I be more loving, to you?
How can I be more kind?

To the Mother of My Love —

Is it wrong to know love?

—

We seed kindness in the soil,
And make it grow in our hearts,

We rise up rhizomes from the ground,
We dust them down and kiss them,

We form orchid to become-wasp and
Wasp to become-orchid.

—

I became your daughter above the sky;
Thunder clouds, my only jewels.

—

My heart is like a bramble-vine
That swathes its ripest fruit.

My heart is like a rolling-tide
That quenches ocean mute.

My heart is like a conifer-seed
That millenniums into tree.

My heart is surer than all these
Because he you made for me.

—

Is it wrong to know love?

Because I love your son.
Your son is kind.

Passion | *Passione*

the farther away
the closer you are

sweet poison
in my blood
welled deep
within my heart

sanguine
as amaranth

Soars of the Monarchs

as tenderheart leaf
of the milkweed
grows my love for you

dusk to dusk
dawn to dawn

rippling and rising
like the monarchs

it soars and soars
it soars and soars

Her Delicate Rose

Behind her widening eyes,
the rose shone red
as a dark vein of his blood.

It was all an illusion,
but not for her.

It was space and time,
measured by her heart.

—

Granados, *Escenas Poéticas*, Book I – III.
'Danza de la Rosa'

TEARS OF THE POET

You're the only man I've ever met
    who seems to have the faintest conception
    of what I mean when I write something.

My poems, I think,
    are merely your voice speaking.

Is not poetry a secret language —
    a *sigh* answering a *sigh*?

We go in and out of each other's minds
    without any effort.

I awaken with you at every dawn
    and listen to you endlessly.

Poem after poem we lie in each other's thoughts, and
    all my teardrops turn into violets.

O PERFECT LOVE

lowly we kneel
our heavenly bodies

i know the soft hymns
his soul likes the most

he is the keystone
anchored inside me

a love without end crowned
by hawthorn and rose

I am Yours, a Soulful Avowal

Having found you, there is
    no moment in my life more significant,
    no barrier I would not overcome to reach you,
    no restraint upon the power of my love.

I have never fully opened myself
    to any human being, and having found you,
    my soul opened wholly to yours.

You are my calm, my other-self, my good light.

I am bound to you,
    not by vow, nor by will, nor by law,
    but by divine grace.

God knitted together our souls, and
    only He knows how much I love you.

I am not my own —
    I am yours.

The Prudent Gardeners

Let us not grow together.
　　Let us grow apart.

I will give you space to stretch your tendrils.
　　You will heed my deciduous tendencies.

Our suns will rise and sink.
　　Our roots will tangle and rich.

Shining a light *here*
　　Will require casting a shade *there*.

Our sky will be a little bluer;
　　Our bed a little greener.

How lovely to tend each other's bloom!

Fresh air within our garden
　　Will make sweet fragrance flow.

Draw me after you, my love. Let us run!

Freeform Haiku of a Fair Argument

sleep repellant
the mind cold-brews
another starbuck's shot

nearness
rubs frayed souls
like dry lightning

dandelion me down to the bare necessities
weed weed weed weed

i will flatten-out
your ten-thousand fold
origami bird

every lovely memory
bruises tender skin
like hailstones

only silent lips
hear twittering birdsongs

i smell your mind
a lingering dew
warm drops of pine

the color of contentedness is sage

PLATONIC RHETORIC

I've got you now,
within me.

Lymph and mirth
no longer
my own.

Where *logos, thymos, eros*
intertwine —
your soul
within
my soul.

Ours is the child of
Poros and Penia,
lack and plenty.

Forever wanting,
yet possessing everything;
we live
in the between.

Freely chosen,
divinely given —
our *theia mania*.

Agape, eros, philia
playfully converge
within us.

Neither
friends nor lovers,
transcending both.

Together
we sit atop
Diotima's ladder.

Eternally one.

By Heaven | 上邪

by heaven
we will be together
forever without end

till mountains crumble and oceans dry
winter thunders and summer snows

overhead the stars
shift and sparkle like
hangzhou city at midnight

high atop mount tianmu
i can only see your smile

even as heaven and earth collide
we will be together
forever without end

—

2000-year-old Chinese Folk Poem

Trap of the Poetess

Let me try to catch him in a little fume of words;
    a bitter fragrance rises from a sonnet
    fragile as the sanity of the birds.

I grow too tired for poetry; too wild
    the mind too faint the flesh; let him
    surrender his spirit and rhetoric; let
    his calm ensnare him, his spirit fly!

    ...this poem is about you; do you know yourself?...

The clarity of his Hellenic mind
    I meant to rouse him till his flesh divined.

Like a man of sense,
    of his impenetrable reticence,
    stares at my passion with a mild surprise.

I burn in pleasant incense for his praise,
    remembering the spilled honey of our days,
    in sacrificial torture at his shrine.

Unwary thirst within my withering brain,
    where he has lain dreaming all these hours,
    sipping honey from the serpent-flowers;
    I weave words where rational men dare not fly.

Yes, I know: the angels disapprove this art of womankind,
    sonnets from my store of softly rhyming sighs.
    But all that I want is the look of his mouth and eyes.

Somehow I do not think that God would mind.

—

Cento of Joy Davidman to C.S. Lewis

Everything

all we
ever had
was *everything*

WATER TO WINE

water to vine
vine to fruit
fruit to seed
seed to root

—

bone to earth
earth to fruit
fruit as child
child as fruit

—

god of truth
truth of you
you to mine
water to wine

A Simple Gift

a simple gift
to see a soul
to bow and bend
pure love bestow

—

to turn and turn
we come round right
to turn and turn
a blessed life

Caelo Marique

sky and sea—
my everything

SKY AND SEA | *Caelo Marique*

Waves, quietly murmuring;
    Among the undulating greenness,
    an ardent longing grows.

See how beautiful the sea is, making me daydream?
    The sky kisses the wave; the wave kisses the sky.

Sky and sea burn together in vestal hope.

A few grains of parched sand — how they slip through my
    fingers! Like shells in an hourglass,
    so lulls this day in my life.

Yes, I'm only midlife today.
    Time has only begun, and the lagoon is deep.

I will wait for you here. Time cannot call back my wave that
    found its shore and died in that embrace.

I am Content

I am content to breathe
the same blue air as him;

Content that over us each night
the same canopy of stars shines dim.

I do not wish to stop the sea
nor set fires to the earth.

I am content to feel his love
as music of my mirth.

ALL THIS WAS ME

A firefly was flickering for you to notice it.

A wave washed toward you out of the sea, or
    as you hiked upon a snowy mountain,
    a tiny sparrow yielded itself to your hearing.

All this was me.

Without lips, I called your name,
    and I made my way to you, without legs.

You never arrived in my arms,
    so I held you with my heart.

I came to you not in dream,
    but in contemplation of reality
    I carry within me.

I had nowhere else to go except inside you.

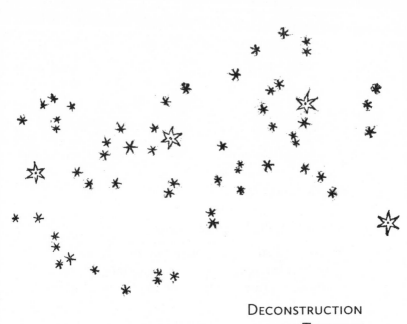

DECONSTRUCTION
OF TWILIGHT

all alone

with you
in dream

i come
undone

and burst
into stars

Celestial Silence

a star spoke to a star

silently coupling in
momentary brilliance

as two souls
light-years apart

together burned

Meditations Written on Lonely Beaches

I. The Shoreline

i am a wave and you are my shore

adrift in the prevailing current
i roam restless upon dark sea

but tidal currents do shift

someday
i will flow naturally into your arms
tranquilly quelled
within the sanctuary of your embrace

II. The Shells

i listen to
seashells in December
laughing amid waves
tiny Fibonacci spirals
reflecting God's full grace
as if a million shimmery mirrors
mimic back your smiling face

III. The Oyster

of the
seven and one half
quintillion
grains of sand
only you could
seed my pearl

IV. The Mangroves

foul saline swamp
of brownish tea
fertile nursery of fragile souls
i do not seek crystal clear life
i much prefer your muck

V. The Tidal Pool

for ages, i couldn't breathe

until churning undercurrents
mixed with gentlest calms
loosened my soul like sea water

releasing myself from others
revealing myself to you

CREATIONISM, ACCORDING TO RUMI

In the beginning,
    I was apart from you,
    and this world did not exist,
    nor did any other.

Then, like the sea,
    you flooded me as a lover,
    and I married you, quickly.

Tidewater goaded our wave
    to break its shore,
    and spiny urchins passionately
    sowed like wild darlings.

We were born into color.
    We became another sky.

A blundering albatross
    landed upon our shoulders
    and for some reason,
    became ours.

There can be no edges
    to our loving now.

Veil of the Jellyfish

An indefinable essence, a numberless life;
    I float upon the abyss of infinite sea.

I am time-space filled with talents —
    sentient, poisonous, luminous.

I am the serene light of a pale moon,
    the golden fleck of a distant star,
    the fiery cloud that drifts in sunrise.

I am your veil of life
    connecting heaven and earth.

I am woman.
I am wife.

Nights by the Sea

We sleep together, you and I,
    next to the sea, upon the shore,
    wild and sweet, lying side by side,
    between pleasure and rest, between air and fire.

All earth conspires to bring you to me,
    as if all matter —
    stars, wind, sand, atoms
    — were tiny strings pulling you toward
    the sheltered isle of my arms.

The wail of the waves,
    the cry of the gull,
    the rustle of the palm,
    everything recognizes us.

We were rooted together in the earth
    and we alone did not know we must grow together;
    our roots were planted in silence.

Lying side by side, we intertwine,
    end upon end, flesh within flesh.

We have found each other thirsty
    and sucked up all the tidal pools.

We devour each other as famished morsels,
    inflicting luscious wounds for shared flesh to grow.

We sleep together, you and I,
    upon the moonlit shore, shy and luxurious.

I ripple when you touch me,
    like a childish river running home.

I crest as the waves. I flow as the monsoon tides.

Sunk within the sandy hook of your arm,
    I can rest, my love, caressed by
    the humid heat of mangroves
    and the misty fog of morning.

I taste the salts of your skin;
    I breathe the smells of your work.

My body blooms as the algae,
    peacefully floating upon you as the foam.

We sleep together, you and I,
    shyly obscene, with bodies cogged together
    as pieces of a well-oiled dream.

I wear you beneath my skin all night,
    lascivious bones pressing against insisting sea,
    legs heaving, spiraling under you,
    and around you, eternal. I am the hugging shore.

Sunrise weeps for us across dark horizon.
    The breeze carries your kiss to me, moistened with
    spray, sewing our mouths together, knitting salt into
    breath, weaving sand into souls.

Listen, my love;
    the sea sings only for you and I.

All the ocean roars in our bodies,
    clouds chime the sky,
    and a soft hymn fills the world;
    as if I can never sleep except with you;
    as if I can only sleep when I dream.

THE WOMAN WHO FELL IN LOVE WITH THE MOON

she found
the sea of tranquility
in oceanic eyes

she felt
the softness of shadow
on bleakest nights

in the fierceness of his stubble
the tenderest glow

he moved her
from afar
as surely as
moontide

and that's all
that mattered

Color of When

Waiting, entirely composed of expectation.

My life's tapestry hues in raw complacency —
    turmeric roots, fresh tarragon, and plum
    — numbly sewn together beneath
    a grateful veil of onyx and ivory thread.

Veil lifted, and now, I know color;
    this warmth of soul's requitance
    like the feeling of
    being near you,
    without ever
    being near you.

It is a pained reaction *–an unraveling–*
    knowing nothing has happened,
    yet all has happened,
    a vivid splitting of light,
    needing nothing more.

I can never revert to black and white again.

I know color now *–our color–*
    a kaleidoscopic frisson,
    a blue hope of sky,
    a wait without when.

Waiting, entirely composed of expectation —
    our *when* is forever-colored *now*.

THE KICK GALVANIC

you cannot hold me
i am the sea

a Protean wave
a Mercurial creed

i flow in you
galvanically

you cannot hold me
i am the sea

Amor Insanus

crazy love—
preferably naked

Waiter, Waiter, Percolator
(Medley of the Ink Spots)

We three: you, my java, and me.

If I didn't care, would my every cup begin and end
    with just your name?

All we have is in these beans.

Poor, no one is poor,
    long as the java is sure,
    in life's cup of dreams.

I don't want to set the pot on fire.
    I just want to be the caffeine in your heart.

A Boring Dream of Our Life in Fine Detail

We'd have a library.

With real books, and real paper,
    none of this electronic shit.

And we'd read aloud to each other,
    or silently, it really wouldn't matter,
    because we'd be *together*, in *our* library,
    and that's the empyreal point.

Just five rooms:
    a kitchen, a bathroom, a bedroom, a sunroom,
    and a huge ass library.

No closets.

That's all we need.

Love Letter From Sea Otter to Snowy Owl

Perhaps I am unwise for you.
Maybe *shellfisharians* and *rodentarians* shouldn't mix.

You probably even think me
overly curious and too furry.

Sure, I know that you are
the quiet studious type,
without time for my playful tricks
and prankish frivolities.

That I would always be admiring you
from under the kelp, always watching you
regurgitate lemmings from afar.

I get it. We're both pragmatists.

And I can respect your brooding solitude
and have seen your protective claws.

But even with those sharp talons
and those solitary nocturnal flights,
I remain decidedly *thick-furred* about you.

And there is no *weaseling* with me.

Every time I think of you,
I floatback *kelpishly*,
otterly charmed.

So I say leave the cold tundra
and fly over the sea to me.

Because your majestic shadow
soaring high above me
is all I need.

FORTUNE COOKIES IN BED

An unlit candle frightens no monkeys, but
    Passion once ignited cannot be snuffed out.
    Bask in the warmth without falling in the flame.
    Over-thinking destroys the magic.

You can't steal second base,
    If you keep your foot on first.

If you can't stop the wave,
    You might as well surf it.

Exit the buffet when you run out of duck sauce.
    Squeeze the orange to find the juice.
    Pluck the flower before it's fully blossomed.
    Irritate the oyster to elicit the pearl.

Allow compassion to guide your decisions.
    Women may find it difficult to resist your
        persuasive manner.

Quick wits fix sticky situations.
    If you seek perfection, you must sharpen your tool.
    Dedicate yourself with a calm hand.
    Utilize your talent for getting things organized.

When the heart is pure, the mind will be clear.
  Flexibility will be the key to success.
  Never underestimate the power of human touch.
  Your greatest obstacle may be my naiveté.

Affairs of the heart shall bring deeply felt joy.
  Laugh long, loud, and often.
  It is smart to prepare for the unexpected.
  The brightest blazes of joy are kindled from the
    most unlikely sparks.

The early bird gets the worm,
  But the second mouse gets the cheese.

An infinite capacity for patience is always rewarded.
  Open your heart, and kiss your ass goodbye.

Conscience is a man's compass, but
  Man who eat fortune cookie alone,
  Get lousy dessert.

—

"In Bed" Fortune Cookie Game

The
best
way
to
practice
love
is
sex.
wait,
wait,
oh
gosh,
typo
alert.
i
meant
patience.
the
best
way
to
practice
love
is
patience.
yes.
patience.
forget
the
sex,
and
replace
sex
with
patience.
silly me.
what
was
i
thinking?!?

From Your Nakedness, a Poem

you streak inside my mind

where no one sees you
but most certainly I do

and your taunting tight ass
becomes this poem

Dinner of the Iguanas

Do you remember that time
the marijuana got into the enchiladas?

We were dining together
on a moonlit beach in Roatán,

and after a shot or two of tequila,
I was inclined to dalliance.

You remained your usual
paragon of virtue,

until you charged at me
like a bull lizard on a rampage.

I've never laughed so hard!

We didn't need any truth.
We needed what ought to be truth.

So we licked each other
under the palapa
waiting for the sun.

FRIED SWEETBREADS WITH DILL POLLEN ON PICKLED WATERMELON RIND

if i could eat you

> i'd take thymus
> spiced and swollen
> in osmotic shock
>
> an antigenic induction
> of self-tolerance
> of positive selection
> of apoptotic purification
>
> this human desire for recognition
> with warty excrescences
> all nodal and oozed
> in warrior-like proliferation
>
> your medullary bastion
> of thymocytic protection
> of hot feisty spiritualness
> of sweet virtuous passion
>
> a rustic dish, humble and pure
>
> you'd make a creamy morsel
> seasoned perfectly and fried crisp
> served with freshness and delicacy
>
> i'd soak you in brine
> poach you in milk
> pan-fry you up

if i could eat you

MANACONDA

In hot throes of passion,
I refuse to utter *schlong.*

Ditto that for *one-eyed-jack,*
Or *knob,* or *wang,* or *dong.*

Dick was like my dad's best friend;
Willy was the rascally neighbor.

Mister Pickle? Trouser Snake?
Are you a kids' cartoon on cable?

Please excuse unhoneyed lip,
My flatter-lack demeanor, but...

I won't "play with *Little Jimmy,*"
and will "never tweet your *weiner.*"

I am just a naïve girl,
not some kāmasūtra genius.

So tell me manly-man,
Can I just scream out for *penis?*

Identity Theft

and you do your thing
and i do my thing

and you are you
and i am i

then comes our thing
and our thing takes everything

then i am you
and you are me

and we are we

Sporting the Sparrow

The go-between brings gifts of
    betel nut and lotus
    declaring undeniable attraction.

Bathed in attar rose,
    adorned in bangles,
    I lie in wait,
        the heat of blush
        hidden amidst thighs.
    I burn,
        and cannot be consumed,
        unquenchable,
        though I monsoon.

Come for me,
    my darling, and
    straddle my mind.

Roving hands unleashed,
    around, behind, between, below.

Embraced as milk and water.
    Marked breast with peacock's foot.
    A pressed kiss arouses
        a tender bitten lip.

Subjugate me deeply
        with arris and mango
        hidden in the sisu trunk.
    Lie still, and I shall
        milk you with pompoir.

In loving congress,
    we shall gingerly water
    the perfumed garden.

United,
    with indivisible oneness,
    eliciting my sparrow's sighs.

CONJUGATION, IN LATIN

amā!
tĕ ămo
ămāmus invĭcem
nōs cēdāmus amori
est sine quā nōn
vāde mēcum
fŭtŭēmus

love!
I love you
we love one another
we surrender to love
it is absolutely necessary
go with me
we will fuck

Maxim of the Pogonophile

A vigorous beard,
with sure probability,
all women revere,
as proof of virility.

Manful potency
as masterful kissers
requires fecundity
with voluminous whiskers.

A Handkerchief for Pavo

your voice reverberating in my brain
sends chills throughout my body

to drown the sound of missing you
— prolific Pavarotti

his voice divine subdues my mind
his debonair suave and haughty

but alas humble beard
brings me to tear

then I can hear but you
— not Pavarotti

A Little Love Drunk

Drinking you in *bittle lottles*.
    Wanting you in *sulping gips*.

Numbing gets me into *trobble*.
    And I only like you *lottle bits*!

And *nuffink* - wait wait wait
    - *nuffink* you can do *'boutit*!

Is We Is, or Is We Ain't?

Is we is,
or is we ain't,
'n luv?

F'sure dawlin'
we do
dat hoodoo
so well.

Dat tarot deck
stacked,
honeychile!

Flippin' dem
Ace of Cups
an' dem Lovers.
Oh lordy, lordy!

We's gots
da ya-ya
an' da mojo
an' da juju.

Cuz we'z
'n luv.

MISIDENTIFICATION OF PORCUPINE

I am not a porcupine
though manly hands recoil.
My hair is soft as silken thread;
my skin, perfumed like a pearl.

Man's vermicious squirming
heralds a quickish *let-'er-go*—
a codfish's shallow shrug;
a cringe-worthy barbed cajole.

Coital unpersuasion,
salvos firing branch to branch.
All touch devoid of tenderness,
thick-skin pricks side-ways glance.

Sharp shoots of rocket piddle,
demonstratous of manpower,
exude testosterosity of
a Trump*esque* golden shower.

Yet once or twice man held me
for cautious procreative sex, and
my children came out children,
not peculiar porcupettes.

Scientifically nonplussed,
men speak *mamby-pamby* jest:
they say they cannot hold me—
hire a pro-trained cuddlist!

Reluctantly resided
to human-touch hiatus,
perhaps I should play opossum
wielding shrieks of quilled coitus?

But I am not a porcupine,
all prickled, barbed, and cruel—
I am not a porcupine.
I am a woman, you fool!

Invective Against Dead Squids

Dead squids,
however fun they may be to throw,
rarely solve any problems.

Sometimes dead squids
are not enough.

Sometimes you
need hugs.

Dibs

evoking the most powerful
law in the universe, *i call dibs.*

i claim the part of you
that you hide
from everyone else.

no take-backs.
your perpetual shotgun.
lick-it-like-i-stole-it.
forever mine.

Subject: Cake No. 50

i want you to always look at me
like it is your birthday
and i am the cake

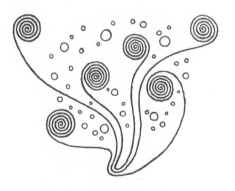

DON'T BURY THE BOURBON

Don't bury the bourbon.
Bring on the rain.

True love is sacrifice,
sufferin',
pain.

Don't bury the bourbon.
Things ain't gotta' be bright.

Swiggin' love's bottle
is the delight.

In Praise of the Femme Fatale

I. Eve

Be dazzled and be damned—
all humanity depends upon it.

II. Mati Hari

Secretly
I am both a
kindergarten teacher
and Javanese princess.

III. Salammbô

Beneath the Zaïmph of Tanît,
quiver a thousand curves
and rhythms of my body.

IV. Cleopatra

Uncorseted and unashamed,
love arrives, wrapped in a rug.

V. Salomé

Dim veils hide soft bosom's charms,
Floating freely, toward open arms;
Veils unfurl as feverish mists,
To reveal God's jewels:
my amethysts.

VI. Me

I am not a woman.
I am your world.

ANGEL OF LIGHT

my black nightgown
more black than gown

slips ever-so-shyly
off bare shoulder

thin straps
dangling precariously
upon pert nipple

taut silk
clinging tightly
upon lush curves

before slinking down
sheepishly to the floor

exposing all
that is good in me

my darling,
I do not
masquerade
in righteousness

i really
am bad

Freudian Slips Of(f) the Thong

O thong, bad thong. You feel so wrong!
Betwixt mo(i)st cracks you tightly cling.
Blistered red, I feel your st(r)ing.

Squished together, (f)a'int my heart.
(S)lips together, (ch)eeks apart.

Riding up in hide-a-way,
my snatch in pub(l)ic exposé!

Scantly clad elastic tightest,
Showing off my b(r)e(a)st and brightest.

Bralci pearl are (s)lightly merrier
(f)licking cross (c)litoral area.
But even (m)oral strands of bead
cannot negate the s(p)ores you knead.

Must I endure your cutting flesher
as orga(ni)sm of erotic-pressure?
Would men think me very (b)anal,
to denounce your pleasure carnal?

I suppose (se)men do perspire
for the (st)iffness you inspire.
But prancing 'round in vivisection
cannot be worth (a)roused erection.

My curves (al)lure in négligée
of Leavers lace loomed in Calais.
So thong you really must now go,
no more (s)p(r)ain, just commando.

And since,
my (c)rack makes poor display,
I'll wear but(t) my smile as lingerie.

Going thongless may seem crass
But men still seem to love my (s)ass!

Pluit et Lucet

*it rains and
it shines*

His Thistles

All she could do
was wait for his rain.

It never came.

She planted dahlias
so thistles would not grow,
but without rain,
dahlias would not grow.

So thistles grew,
thorned and noble,
and the goldfinches and
fritillary butterflies came,
humbled and pained.

He brought more love
than she'd ever known,
when his thistles came.

THINGS WE'VE NEVER KNOWN

How can I miss
the things we've never known,

like lips we've yet to kiss, and
hands that hold like home?

I reminisce our garden flowers, yet
our seed remains unsown.

I wonder how I miss
these things we've never known.

Uncommon Sense

I can't tell rhyme from reason,
or if *Whispering Hope* is true.
My only predilection
on this earth is you.

I clutch your image inchly,
brave hope, and dare all costs.
Our thrilled ideal swirls me surreal.
All common sense is lost.

Metaphors for a Long Marriage

I. The Ficus Tree

I keep trying to kill it,
but it's never looked lovelier.

II. The Marathon

Suffice to say, this is the grueling stretch,
where one must dig-in for those last hellacious miles.

III. The Railway Tracks

Always side by side, but never coming any closer.

IV. The Cliff Divers

Plunging from highest highs to deepest lows—
    paired jumps must be precisely timed,
    to synchronistically hit the lagoon,
    without splattering upon the rocks.

V. The Chameleons

When did *I* change? Look at *you*!

VI. The Sunshowers

Rain is falling while the sun remains shining.

VII. The Finite Series

Nobody can do this *forever, forever, forever, forever,* death.

VIII. The Fox's Wedding

As far as anyone can tell,
this is a perfectly normal marriage.

VINEGAR AND HONEY

Words as plums in silence strung;
    Writing poems to each other's eyes.

Love grants us powers that nature might deny.

We make oceans of plums,
    and sink them (tears) like ships.

Whatever has happened, bitter or sweet,
    all was done for love.

Now the life in our body,
    the light in our eyes,
    the blood in our heart,
    is but one.

We are half vinegar, half honey.

Whiskey in a Teacup

I am Soft, with approachable curves,
    body molding effortlessly
    within a man's arms.
    A silk chemise. A goose down pillow. A buttery cookie.

I am Hard, with a carbon fiber soul,
    clement, with fairness and justice,
    unbreakable, as a cast-iron skillet.
    I can forge a man with mere femininity.
    A scaffold. A mother's arms. A knife-sharpener.

Good am I, as a dimpled cherub,
    with angelic sweetness,
    minding her P's and Q's,
    never misstepping, while
    sipping life's perfection.
    A prized-possession. A halo of light. A rare vintage.

Sharp and Sage, I am,
  naming each tree's phylogeny,
  without ever overlooking the forest's grandeur.
  I see clearly, acting only with prudence,
  bravely pouncing, whenever required.
  A wily tigress. A precocious child. A Russian chess master.

I am Passion, with pure white blood,
  like a campfire fueled by nitromethane.
  I can melt steel, and freeze lava.
  I trade joy as currency,
  arbitraging pleasure for pleasure.
  A Greek goddess. A dahlia bouquet. An Alabama firework.

I am a woman in love —
  Drink me in slowly, as if sipping firewater.
  Within me lies a burning cauldron
    A double Oban neat.
  daintily contained inside this prim and proper
  rose-pink china.

Vow of Remembrance

i beg you to remember

how flames lick
flames enfold
flames loop our veins

how creation rushes around us
molten and shy and sweet

how in each other's presence
we are utterly consumed

i beg you to remember

Quando

When the multiplication of the universe
    turns all blue hope into stars;

When time trembles and passes us by,
    and our lightning no longer burns;

When flower by flower, breath by breath,
    wave by wave, you erase my name;

When you weep like a damp night in Havana,
    and cackle like an old silly fool;

When our glass house of infinite tenderness
    shatters around us like a jar;

When little by little you gingerly pluck-out
    my roots from the kind soil of your heart;

When like chocolate's bittersweetness,
    you trade our love for something new;

When you foolishly forget me—

                I will still sail and sleep
                upon your name.

              I will wait as an empty house
         until you come and dwell inside me,

          until you remember me as home
          and we fall together like stones
              upon our hearth.

The Common Prayer for Stillness

I lock the door and
kneel down on the chair,
bowing down my head to my knees
in a convulsion upon the floor.

In a convulsion—because I love him.

I double myself up in a convulsion
with my head fallen upon the chair
— because I love him.

It is far more like pain, like agony,
than like prayer.

I sway myself back and forth in spasms
of unbearable feeling
— because I love him.

And taking a pillow from the bed,
I crush it against myself and
sway myself unconsciously
in sharp gasps of unbearable feeling.

Right in my womb I feel it—
the terrible unbearable feeling
of malignant incompleteness
of unfathomable love.

How can I bear it.

I kneel upon floor in a convulsion,
weeping bitterly,
tremulous and weak,
writhing in pain,
— because I love him.

I weep upon the chair
until I become still,
until calmness covers me like sleep—
an eternity of dreamless black slumber.

I wait for this stillness
and thank God
— because I love him.

In pure stillness,
I resolve and get up.
I smooth my hair, dry my face.

I am light, ethereal, so distant, so still.
I feel that nothing, nothing can ever touch me.

Then I unlock the door and
return to my living
— because I love him.

No Birdsong

I sang not a note my whole life
Until I found the sharpest thorn,

The perfect thorn
To impale myself upon,

Singing happily as I died
The sweetest song
Ever heard.

—

I loved you most
When most in pain.

Better a thorn bird, living or dead,
Than no birdsong at all

Sonnet No. 226 — Leitmotif

Descend O love! Spiteful time is bitter foe.
Tristan's dissonant chord lingers unresolved.
As apogee of tension pulls vines beloved,
Untrammeled souls in ardent rapture grow.

Honeysuckle and hazel do intertwine
In cacophonic pitch of *langsam* desire.
A single bond of *schmachtend* breath require
Dual insistence of harmonic twist—divine!

Floating, without melodic resolution,
Chromaticism grounded in heaving swell.
Inosculation of notes and roots taunt Hell.

Discordance heralds prophetic cessation,
Raptured in suspense of love's calming quell—
Either by death, or delayed gratification.

—

Wagner: *Tristan und Isolde,* WWV 90

The Languish of Flowers

I. Queen of the Andes

if I bloom only once
in this lifetime
I am glad I bloomed
for you

i merely ask
for us to bloom
together
before i
wither and die

II. Dandelions

from love's single fruition
spills a million seeds
endearments of perfection
or propagating weeds?

III. Lupines

i know
this is a love poem,
not a botany lesson,
but you must choose;
    your lupines
    or your life?

and remember,
i'm your lupines

IV. CAVENDISH BANANAS

virgin flower
of seedless wonder
has not had sex
for 10,000 years

proving abstinence
can be delicious

V. SAFFRON CROCUS

many, many flowers
flavor my basmati
red tips only
all stigma, no style

VI. MOONFLOWERS

we will bite
the poisonous apple-peru
awakening delirious
in the brocade of dawn
to trumpets of
morning glories

for who can fault
the purity of our
night-blooming cereus?

miracles opening only
in the darkest corners
of love

THE YELLOW WALLPAPER

There are things in my mind
that nobody knows but me.

A slight hysterical tendency —
but what is one to do?

I did write for a while,
in spite of him.

But only so I could get well faster.

He laughs at me, of course,
but one expects that in marriage.

He says that my habit of story-making is
sure to lead to all manner of excited fantasies.

If only I were well enough to write a little more,
perhaps it may relieve this press of ideas and calm me?

But he says I ought to use
my will and good sense to control
these imaginative tendencies.

So I try.

I don't even know why I should write.
I don't want to. I don't feel capable.

I am convinced that
writing is a bad habit because you see,
I can no longer sleep.

And that cultivates deceit, for I don't dare tell him
I'm awake - oh no! I lay silently still
and watch the moonlight.

I cry at nothing,
and I cry most of the time.

Of course I don't when he is near,
or anybody else,
but when I am alone.

And I am alone a good deal now.

Here he comes —
   I should put this away!
He hates to have me write a word.

He is very careful and loving,
and hardly lets me think without special direction;

Because he is so wise, and
because he loves me so.

He knows there is no reason for my suffering,
and that satisfies him.

But I'm getting dreadfully
fretful and querulous without my writing.

The fact is
I am getting a little annoyed of him too.

I have locked the bedroom door
and thrown the key down the path.

The key is down the back path, under the redwood tree,
I tell him in the gentlest, calmest voice.

And then I say it again, several more times,
very gently and slowly, and
so very often that, *eventually*,
he will have to go and look.

You see, there are things in my mind
that nobody knows but me.

I want to astonish him.

Then Came His Thunder

What man hath joined together
God can rip asunder.

He struck me with you.
Then came His thunder.

And if We had a Week — or Two

And if we had a week — or two —
    allowing ourselves to simply be —
        what would we make of it?

> *what we are is ours*
> *what we create is ours*

Are we not resourceful and intelligent persons—
    whereas now — *caged?*

And if we made time and space to be together —
    allowing ourselves to simply be — to touch
        each other without comment or possession —

> *a hand upon a hand*
> *an ankle around an ankle*

Would we not open ourselves unconditionally

> *to breathe side by side*
> *to hold each other's time*
> *without demand or plan?*

And if we had a week —or two —
    to remake our world by living in it,
        defining what words mean for us —

> *not anybody's earth, or anybody's sun*
> *but our earth, our star, our mountain*

Could we not find a small space
    for a limited time in which to marvel
        in what we have found in each other?

How much love could we share —
    if we had a week — or two?

Chopin's Heart

As Chopin's heart,
Festered in a jar;

Submerged in a dark-amber
Liquor, thought to be cognac;

Massively enlarged and floppy,
With a frosted appearance;

Separated from body,
Which rots in Père Lachaise;

As Chopin's heart,
Drunken and swollen,

I touch my piano
As I cannot touch you.

—

Prelude Op. 28 No. 4 in E Minor, 'Suffocation'

To My Husband Upon Vicennial Introspection—

Because you let
my eye rolls slip;

Because you indulge
my *capriciosity*;

This is the time of our lives.

No simpered biopic.
No histrionic vibes.

Think of how many cups of coffee
we never drank together.

Think of how prolonged marriage
causes colon cancer.

All marriages end tragically —
Either you split up or someone dies.

It's really this tricky middle bit that matters.
And remember, my love:
    Irritation is *not* an argument.

The dahlias in the dahlia-garden
are mine and mine only.

Everything else is ours.

But these are mere public avowals. Let me surmise:
    It's good to be us.

Variations on Love in F# Minor

I. Schumann, Bunte Blätter, Op 99
Albumblätter 1. *Ziemlich langsam*

O soaring owl,
How are you content and calm?
Do you not see how the storm surrounds us?

II. Grieg, Des Dichters Herz, 'The Poet's Heart' Op 52 No 3

I know solid ground
and lucid, unshakeable melodies;

But I know
that the storm is the source
of what I know.

III. Tchaikovsky, Twelve Pieces. Op 40 No 9
Tempo di valse

The tumult of storm is penetrated only
by beams of his smile.

His light plays in her hair
as poetry.

IV. Fauré, Pavane Op 50

The owl majestically lands
among the fragile cedar-limbs.

It was night all afternoon. It was pouring,
and it was going to pour
for the rest of their lives.

NOTES

A Simple Gift is based on the Shaker song *Simple Gifts* by
Elder Joseph Brackett. 1848... 33
The Common Prayer for Stillness is based on, and includes
phrasing from, *The Lost Girl* by D.H. Lawrence. London:
M. Secker, 1920. 92-93
The Yellow Wallpaper is based on, and includes phrasing
from, the short-story of the same title by Charlotte
Perkins Gilman. *New England Magazine.* 1892...... 98-99
Chopin's Heart was inspired by the news article by Quinn.
"Chopin's Heart, Pickled in a Jar, Offers Clues to His
Death," *New York Times.* 6 Nov 2017 with descriptive
phrasing from Witt, Michał, et al. "A closer look at
Frederic Chopin's cause of death." *The American Journal
of Medicine* 131.2. 211-212. 2018. 102

All artwork is reprinted from the public domain including:
*Ver Sacrum: Mittheilungen der Vereinigung Bildender
Künstler Österreichs.* Wien: Vereinigung; 1898-1905.
    Josef Maria Auchentaller. 1900 .... 11, 31
    Koloman Moser. 1899-1901...................... 14, 18, 54, 75, 82
    Fanny Zakucka. 1902... 24
    Leopold Bauer. 1902... 36
    Alfred Roller. 1900.. 50
    Josef Hoffmann. 1903.. 61, 77
    Jutta Sika. *Owls.* 1903...................................... 105
Jugend. München: G. Hirth's Verlag. 1896-1940.
    Unkown. 1908 17
    Neureuther. 1904.. 97
Sidereus Nuncius (Starry Messenger). The Pleiades.
    Galileo Galilei. 1610.. 40-41
Deutsche Kunst und Dekoration. Darmstadt: A. Koch.
    Heinrich Vogeler, 1902.. 44
University of Delaware Library. Wikimedia Commons.
    Rockwell Kent. *Katherine Bush Bookplate.* 1920 56
General Zoology, or Systematic Natural History. George Shaw.
    London: Kearsley. 1826.. 72

if love doesn't hurt,
you aren't doing it right

Made in the USA
Monee, IL
30 June 2020